Getting into Netball

Luke Davis and Damien Davis

MACMILLAN
LIBRARY

First published in 2006 by
MACMILLAN EDUCATION AUSTRALIA PTY LTD
627 Chapel Street, South Yarra 3141

Visit our website at www.macmillan.com.au

Associated companies and representatives throughout the world.

National Library of Australia
Cataloguing-in-Publication data

Davis, Luke, 1983–.
  Netball.

  Includes index.
  For middle to upper primary school aged children.
  ISBN 978 0 7329 9987 2.
  ISBN 0 7329 9987 1.

  1. Netball – Juvenile literature. I. Davis, Damien. II.
  Title. (Series: Getting into (South Yarra, Vic.)).

796.324

Edited by Helena Newton
Text and cover design by Cristina Neri, Canary Graphic Design
Illustrations by Nives Porcellato and Andy Craig
Photo research by Legend Images

Printed in China

Acknowledgements
The author and the publisher are grateful to the following for permission to reproduce copyright material:

Front cover image, Sarah Barrett of the Swifts in action, courtesy of Adam Pretty/Getty Images; inset image of netball
courtesy of Sporting Images.

Australian Sports Commission, p. 22; Mike Hewitt/ALLSPORT/Getty Images, p. 28; Tony Lewis/ALLSPORT/Getty Images,
p. 23; Robert Cianflone/Getty Images, p. 29; Stuart Hannagan/Getty Images, p. 30; Adam Pretty/Getty Images, p. 4;
Michael Steele/Getty Images, p. 5; Newspix/Tony Lewis, p. 26; Photolibrary/Botanica/Constantine Tanya, p. 27;
Sporting Images, pp. 1, 6, 24; © Sport the library/Jeff Crow, p. 7.

While every care has been taken to trace and acknowledge copyright, the publisher tenders their apologies for any
accidental infringement where copyright has proved untraceable. Where the attempt has been unsuccessful, the publisher
welcomes information that would redress the situation.

Disclaimer
The activities described in this book are potentially dangerous, and could result in serious injury if attempted by
inexperienced persons. The authors and publisher wish to advise readers that they take no responsibility for any mishaps
that may occur as a result of persons attempting to perform the activities described in this book.

Contents

Glossary words

When a word is printed in **bold**, you can look up its meaning in the Glossary on page 31.

The game

Netball is an action-packed team sport enjoyed by players of all ages and abilities, from junior players to highly skilled **elite** players. Netball is the most popular sport played by women and girls in Australia. Mixed and all-male netball are also very popular. The national netball competition is known as the National Netball League (NNL) and includes teams from the Australian Capital Territory, New South Wales, Queensland, South Australia, Victoria and Western Australia.

Netball is played in 45 countries around the world, including Australia, England, New Zealand, South Africa and the West Indies. Its popularity is also growing in the United States of America and Canada. At the international level, netball is controlled by the International Federation of Netball Associations (IFNA). The IFNA is responsible for running the World Netball Championships and the International Series, played between the national teams of participating countries.

The history of netball

The sport of netball was adapted from the American game of basketball. Netball was first played in England in 1897, and in 1901, the official rules of netball were developed. Since then, the popularity of netball has grown dramatically and it is now played as both an indoor and outdoor sport in countries all around the world.

Elite netballers are highly skilled athletes.

Playing a match

A netball match is played by two teams of seven players each, on a rectangular court. The players aim to pass the ball up the court to a team-mate inside the **goal circle**, who then shoots for **goal**. The ball needs to be shot through the goal ring from inside the goal circle to score a goal. The winner of a match is the team that scores the most goals. Each team has two main aims. The first aim is to score as many goals as possible, and the second is to stop the opposition team from scoring.

A match consists of four 15-minute quarters. At the end of each quarter, the teams change direction and aim for the goals at the opposite ends of the court. The game is controlled by two umpires, who patrol each side of the court. The umpires use whistles to stop play and award free passes to the opposing team if rules are broken. Netball matches can be played outdoors on non-slip surfaces, such as asphalt, or indoors on sprung wooden floors.

Scoring goals is one of the main aims of netball.

Did you know?

Netball was originally called women's basketball. In the first netball games, the goalposts were made of broomsticks and wet paper bags were attached to the top to act as goals.

Equipment

The equipment used in netball is simple, but it needs to meet the standards set by the sport's governing body.

The ball

A netball is made from lightweight rubber and has an outer coating that provides good grip. A netball is about the same size as a soccer ball, but only weighs about 450 grams and bounces very well. Their design means that netballs are perfect for passing, catching and bouncing.

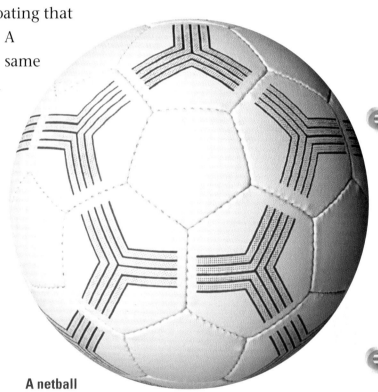

A netball

Mouthguards

Netball is a non-contact sport, however, it is played at a fast pace and it is possible that players will make contact with one another. Players need to wear mouthguards so that they do not damage their teeth if they happen to be bumped, pushed or if they collide with other players.

EQUIPMENT

Clothing

Netball clothing needs to be practical and comfortable. In the past, female netballers have worn a shirt and skirt and male netballers have worn a polo shirt and shorts. Recently, however, elite netballers and some club netballers have started to wear one-piece **lycra** outfits. These suits are very light and do not restrict players' movements. They are very comfortable to play netball in.

Netball outfits come in team colours and have letters attached to the chest and back. These letters indicate the position of the player, and tell the umpire which part of the court the player is allowed to play in.

Runners and socks

Netballers wear runners that are light, comfortable and stable to help support the ankles. Netball runners also have a non-slip tread pattern on the bottom. This makes it easy for netballers to sprint, turn and stop quickly. Netballers wear socks that are soft and well padded to prevent blisters.

Rule
Players must not wear anything that could be dangerous to themselves or another player, including jewellery.

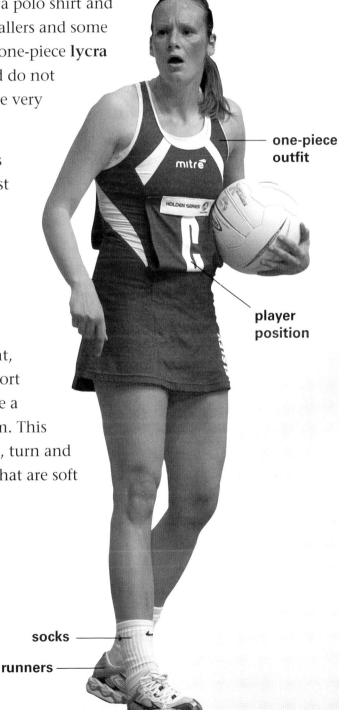

one-piece outfit

player position

socks

runners

The court

Netball is played on a rectangular court with sides that are 30.5 metres long and 15.25 metres wide. At each end of the court is a goal. The goal consists of a goalpost that is 3.05 metres tall, with a goal ring on top. The netball court is divided into three parts. One third is called the **attacking** third, and includes the goal circle and goal that a team is attacking. The centre third includes a centre circle, where the game begins and is restarted after each goal is scored. The **defensive** third is a mirror image of the attacking third and consists of the goal circle and goal that a team is defending.

A netball court

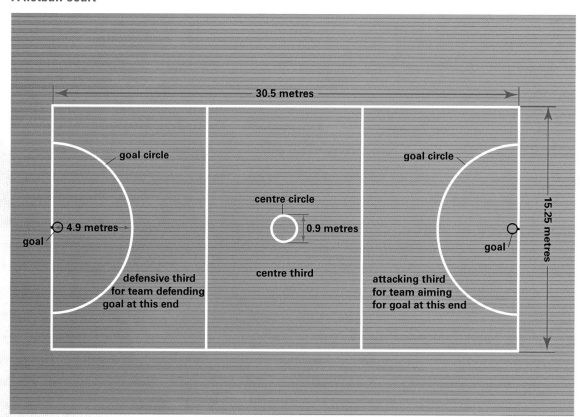

The players

Netball players can play in seven different positions. These include the centre, three **attacking positions** and three **defensive positions**. The centre (C) is one of the most important positions because this player gives and receives so many passes up and down the court. Centres need to be very fast and fit because they have to cover the whole court. The only areas that a centre cannot enter are the two goal circles.

The three attacking positions are the goal shooter (GS), goal attack (GA) and wing attack (WA). The goal shooter and goal attack are the only two players allowed to shoot for goal inside the goal circle. The wing attack supports the centre player in the centre and attacking thirds of the court.

The three defensive positions are the goal keeper (GK), goal defence (GD) and wing defence (WD). The goal keeper and goal defence aim to stop the opposition's goal shooter and goal attack from scoring. The wing defence guards the opposition's wing attack.

This diagram shows the playing areas that each player is allowed in.

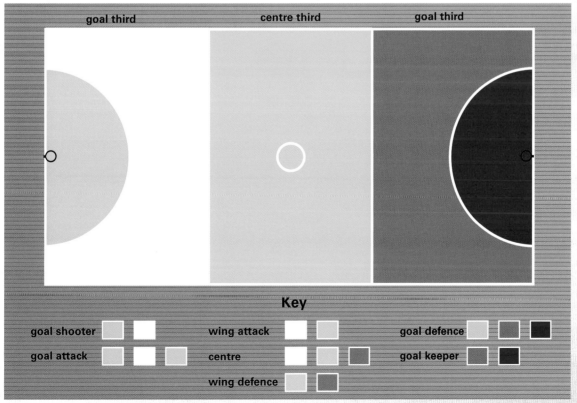

goal third   centre third   goal third

Key

goal shooter	wing attack	goal defence
goal attack	centre	goal keeper
	wing defence	

Netballers use some basic and some more complicated skills. Throughout a netball match, the other players attempt to move the ball to their **shooters** by passing the ball from team-mate to team-mate. Players need to be able to gather and catch the ball well, and to stop the opposition from getting the ball by **intercepting**. With practice, players try to master these skills.

Chest pass

The chest pass is the most basic passing technique, and is used for short, fast passes. To make a chest pass, the player holds the ball in two hands with the fingers and thumbs spread around the ball, and brings the ball into the chest by bending the elbows. The player then transfers the bodyweight forward and lunges with one leg while extending the arms in a pushing motion. Finally, the player 'flicks' the ball forward using the wrists and fingertips.

Rule

When a free pass or shot is awarded, the player who broke the rules must stand next to their opponent until the free pass is made.

Chest passes are best used when a player is not being closely defended.

Shoulder pass

The shoulder pass is a one-handed pass used to cover long distances. While the shoulder pass allows the player to throw the ball a longer distance, it can be harder to control the direction of the pass. To make a shoulder pass, the player follows these steps.

The shoulder pass

1 Holding the ball at shoulder height with one palm underneath, the player turns side-on to the target, with the legs spread apart. Taking the throwing arm back behind the head, the player points at the target with the other hand.

2 Next, the player transfers their bodyweight to the front foot while throwing the ball in the direction of the target.

3 The player follows through with the throwing arm, in the direction of the target.

Lob pass

A lob pass is a high, looping, one-handed pass used to lift the ball over an opponent. It can be used if the player is being blocked by an opponent, or if a team-mate is standing behind an opponent. The lob pass makes the ball travel through the air in a high **arc**. To make a lob pass, the player holds the ball above and behind the head, then extends the throwing arm upwards and in the direction of the target. The player releases the ball with a wrist and finger flick.

A lob pass needs to be accurate so that the opposition players do not have a chance to intercept it.

Bounce pass

If being tightly guarded by a tall opponent, the player may need to use a bounce pass to get the ball to a team-mate. The aim of the bounce pass is to bounce the ball underneath the opponent's arm so that it reaches the team-mate. This technique is only used for short passes. It can be either a one-handed or two-handed pass. If making a one-handed bounce pass, the player begins the pass at hip-height. If making a two-handed bounce pass, the player begins the pass at shoulder-height. To perform a bounce pass, the player follows these steps.

The bounce pass

1 The player aims the pass at a piece of ground that is an appropriate distance away.

2 Bending both knees, the player steps forward while releasing the ball under and around the opponent. The ball bounces underneath the opponent's arm, and into the team-mate's hands.

Side pass

The side pass is another passing technique that can be used when the player is being blocked by an opponent. The aim of the side pass is to use the arms to pass the ball around an opponent's side. The power for this pass comes from the player's shoulders, arms and wrists. To complete a side pass, the player follows these steps.

The side pass

1 The player holds the ball with two hands and positions it at head height.

2 Next, the player draws the ball back behind the head and to one side.

3 Stepping forward, the player leans out to the side of the opponent and extends both arms while passing the ball around the opponent.

Goal shooting

Goal shooting is an important technique because the team with the most goals wins the match. Only the goal attack (GA) and goal shooter (GS) may shoot for goal, and they need to do this from inside the goal circles.

When preparing to shoot for goal, the player stands upright with both arms above the head. The player's feet are a comfortable distance apart. The ball rests on the palm and fingers of the preferred hand, and the player uses the other hand to guide and steady the ball. The player focuses on the goal ring and bends the knees and elbows slightly. As the player shoots, both legs are straightened and the shooting arm is extended upwards. The other hand is used to guide the ball in the right direction. Finally, the player drops the guiding hand away and releases the ball by extending the wrist of the shooting hand.

The player needs to throw the ball high when shooting for goal.

Did you know?

Top netball teams regularly score more than 50 goals in a match. The Australian team has achieved the highest score in a World Championship match. In 1991, they scored 113 goals against Singapore.

Catching

The skill of catching the ball from a pass is just as important as the pass itself. Players need to be able to catch effectively so that their team can maintain possession of the ball and score goals. Before catching the ball, the player moves quickly into a space to receive the ball without having it intercepted. Then the player calls for the pass. To catch the ball, the player follows these steps.

Catching the ball

1 The player focuses on the ball as it approaches and places the hands in the ready position, just in front of the chest.

2 The player reaches out to meet the ball with the fingers spread apart and the thumbs behind the ball for support. As the player grasps the ball, the arms are relaxed slightly before the ball is brought into the chest.

Catching on the run

Netball is a quick game and players often have to catch and pass on the run. To catch the ball on the run, players call out to a team-mate while running and point to a spot where they want to receive the pass. As the ball sails through the air, players need to watch the ball's flight path carefully. They extend both arms with the hands in the catching position and jump slightly into the air to meet the ball. Then they grasp the ball and land back on the court with both knees bent to absorb the impact.

If leading, or running, to the right, players land on the right foot first, and if leading to the left, they land on the left foot first. When receiving a pass on the run, players may not lift the landing foot off the ground until they have passed the ball off again.

The player catches the ball and holds it close to her body if being closely guarded by a defender.

Pivoting

According to the rules of netball, a player cannot take more than one step after gaining possession of the ball. A player may **pivot**, however, to change direction. The rules and technique for pivoting are:

- the pivot foot is the first foot to touch the ground after the player receives a pass or gathers the ball
- the player can change direction and move around by pushing off the ground with the other foot and swivelling on the ball of the pivot foot
- the player cannot drag the pivot foot, and if the pivot foot is lifted to pass or shoot, it cannot be replaced until the pass is made.

Pivoting is very useful if the player is closely guarded. The player can pivot around to get away from an opponent and pass to a team-mate who is free.

After catching the ball, the player can pivot on one foot before passing the ball.

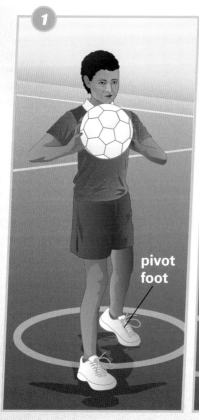

pivot foot

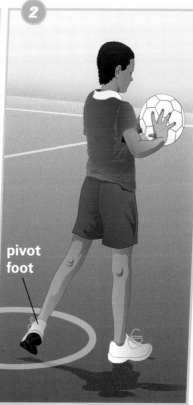

pivot foot

pivot foot

The toss-up

When two players grab the ball or break the rules at the same time, the umpire stops play. To restart play, the umpire conducts a **toss-up**. The two players involved stand roughly a metre apart, facing each other with their hands on their thighs. The umpire holds the ball between the players and flicks it up into the air to shoulder height. When the ball leaves the umpire's hands, both players try to take possession of the ball first.

The umpire conducts the toss-up on the exact spot where the players grabbed the ball or broke the rules.

Throw-in

If the ball goes out of play during a netball match, the team who touched the ball last is penalised and the other team is given a free pass, called a throw-in. The player who is awarded the throw-in stands with their toes next to the sideline and throws the ball back into play without moving their feet.

Defending a pass or shot

If an opponent takes possession of the ball, the player needs to defend by making it difficult for the opponent to successfully pass or shoot. When defending, the aim is to block or intercept the ball, or force the opponent to make an inaccurate pass or shot.

To defend successfully, the player needs to recover quickly when an opponent takes possession of the ball by shuffling back to stand about a metre from the opponent. The player focuses on the ball in the opponent's hands and raises the arms. Then the player leans forward with the arms stretched out and tries to block the throwing arm of the opponent.

The defending player's feet need to be 90 centimetres from the opponent's feet.

Intercepting a throw

If the player can predict where an opponent is going to throw the ball, then they can try to intercept the pass before it reaches its target. Timing is very important when trying to intercept a throw, and to do it successfully the player needs to:

- watch the person throwing the ball closely and focus on the flight of the ball
- push off strongly and run with both arms outstretched
- jump and grab the ball in midair or knock it away from the opponent just as the ball arrives.

Intercepting a throw needs to be timed carefully so that the ball is caught before it reaches an opposing player.

Blocking

Blocking can be used when the opposition has the ball and the player needs to guard an opponent carefully. The player faces the opponent, and stands very close without touching. Staying on the toes, the player tries to shadow the movements of the opponent. If the opponent tries to run into an open space, the player moves to block them.

Blocking makes it difficult for an opponent to move into a good position on the court.

Rules

The game of netball has a number of different rules that players need to be aware of before they begin to play.

A player can take a free throw-in after an opposing player has caused the ball to go out of court.

Offside

Each player on a netball team is allowed in certain areas of the court. If a player is out of that area, the umpire declares the player offside and awards a free pass to the opposition.

Out of court

The ball is considered to be out of court when it has crossed the boundary line, or is in contact with an object or player who is outside the court. The player who last touched the ball before it went out of court is penalised, and a free throw-in is given to the opposition.

Obstruction

Players cannot stand closer than 90 centimetres to a player they are defending. If the defender's feet move within 90 centimetres of their opponent, this is called an **obstruction** and a free pass is awarded to the opposition.

> **Rule**
> The netball code of conduct states that players must accept the decisions of the umpires without question or complaint.

Contact

Players cannot make contact with another player, whether the other player has possession of the ball or not. If a player makes contact with an opponent, a free pass is awarded to the opponent.

Stepping

A player cannot take more than one step after gaining possession of the ball. If they do, it is called 'stepping' and results in a free pass being awarded to the opposition. A player is allowed to pivot on their landing foot to change direction, but if they drag their pivot foot before passing they will be penalised for stepping.

Players need to avoid making contact with one another while playing netball.

Ball control

Players cannot hold the ball for more than three seconds and are not allowed to bounce the ball to themselves. It is also against the rules to throw the ball over a whole third of the court. These three offences result in free passes being awarded to the opposition.

Rule

Players who use bad language or aggressive actions are awarded a penalty. In some cases, players can be suspended.

Scoring and timing

In a netball match, the team that scores the most goals wins. Only the goal shooter and goal attack from each team can shoot for goal. In order for the goal to be counted, the shooter needs to:

- be inside the goal circle when they receive a pass and take a shot
- take the shot within three seconds of catching the ball.

If the shot is missed, the shooter can only catch the ball again if it has bounced off the goal ring.

A netball match consists of four 15-minute quarters, controlled by an official timekeeper. At the end of each quarter, the teams change directions and aim for the goals at the opposite ends of the court. At the end of the hour of play, the team with the most goals is the winner. If the scores are level at the end of play, the match is a draw.

Rule

After each goal is scored, the two teams take turns to restart play with a centre pass.

The goal shooter can score a goal by shooting from inside the goal circle. The goal keeper tries to stop the opposition from scoring.

Umpires

The two umpires wear white uniforms and are in charge of:

- enforcing the rules and making sure that the game is fair
- awarding penalties and free passes when the rules are broken
- deciding when a goal has been scored.

When a rule is broken, the umpire blows the whistle. Then they announce what the penalty was awarded for and which team is being given the free pass. They also blow the whistle after a goal is scored and again when play restarts.

These are some of the signals used by netball umpires.

Pointing one arm to the side signals the direction of the pass.

Holding both hands in front with palms close together signals that a short pass has been made.

Holding both hands in front, palms down, and alternately raising and lowering them signals stepping.

Lifting one palm upwards signals that players need to compete in a toss-up.

Moving one hand in front of the body as if leaping over a hurdle signals that a player is offside or the ball has been thrown over the centre third.

Holding both hands out with a small gap between them signals that a player is obstructing an opponent.

Touching one forearm signals that one player has made contact with another player's arm.

Holding one arm across the body or to the side signals that a player is obstructing an opponent by blocking.

Player fitness

Netball is a physically demanding game. Netballers need to be fit, quick and flexible, and have good heart and lung power. To get the most out of their netball matches, players need to warm up, cool down and develop netball fitness by training.

It is a good idea to begin each netball training session by jogging.

Warming up and cooling down

A netball warm-up consists of a three-minute jog, followed by stretching exercises. A good warm-up gets players' muscles warm and stretched so that they can train and play better. A cool-down stretches the muscles out after training or playing. Players are also less likely to be injured after stretching.

Shoulder stretch

With one hand, the player reaches behind their neck and as far down their back as possible. With the other hand, the player slowly puts pressure on the elbow of the arm that is being stretched. The player holds the shoulder stretch for 30 seconds, then swaps arms.

Leg roll

The player lies on the back with both arms spread wide, one leg straight and one leg bent. Slowly, the player rolls the bent leg across and over the straight leg, keeping the shoulders flat on the ground. The player touches the ground with the bent knee and holds this position for 30 seconds, before repeating the roll to the other side.

Quad stretch

The player stands with one leg straight and the other bent and raised behind. With one hand, the player reaches behind and slowly pulls the foot of the bent leg up towards the buttocks. This stretches the quadriceps muscle, or quad, which is the large muscle on the front of the thigh. The player holds the stretch for 30 seconds, then swaps legs.

Seated hamstring stretch

Sitting with one leg straight and the other leg bent to the side, the player bends forward at the waist and slowly slides both hands down the straight leg as far as possible. This stretches the hamstring of the straight leg, which runs down the back of the thigh and behind the knee. The player holds the stretch for 30 seconds, then swaps legs.

The player holds each stretch, such as the quad stretch, for 30 seconds.

Calf stretch

The player stands close to a wall or fence. Resting both hands on the wall or fence, the player places one leg further back than the other. Keeping the heel of the back foot on the ground and bending the front knee, the player slowly bends both arms and leans in toward the wall or fence. The player feels the stretch in the calf muscle of the straight leg. The player holds the stretch for 30 seconds, then swaps legs.

Trunk stretch

The player lies face-down with both hands under the shoulders and both legs straight. The player slowly straightens the arms and arches the back, keeping both thighs flat on the ground so that the trunk is fully stretched. The player holds the stretch for 30 seconds, then lowers the trunk back to the ground.

Competition

Each year, netball competitions are held in cities and suburbs all over Australia and in 45 other netball-playing nations

Young players can join teams in junior netball competitions.

Local competitions

Netball clubs, schools and local communities organise netball competitions for players of all ages throughout the year. Usually there are two netball seasons: summer and winter. Competitions cater for beginners as well as for more experienced netballers. Each netball club is part of a league, which consists of a number of teams. Throughout each season, the clubs play each other and are awarded points for the number of wins they have. At the end of the season, the top teams play each other in the finals series. This series decides which team wins the competition.

Did you know?

More than 450 000 people of all ages play in the hundreds of netball competitions in Australia each year.

The National Netball League

The National Netball League (NNL) is the leading netball competition in Australia. The National Netball League players are among the best netballers in the country and are fit, strong and skilful. The National Netball League consists of eight teams from all over Australia. Each season, the eight teams play each other twice. At the end of the season, the top teams battle it out in the finals series to find out which team will be awarded the premiership trophy.

The World Championships

The netball World Championships are held every four years and are organised by the International Federation of Netball Associations (IFNA). Teams representing nations from all over the globe compete in this international tournament, which is held in a different country each time. The World Championships are considered to be an extremely important netball tournament. It is seen as a very high honour to represent your country in a World Championship tournament.

Being awarded the premiership trophy is a proud moment for a netball team.

Commonwealth Games

The **Commonwealth** Games is a multi-sport event that is held every four years. Competing athletes represent all the nations of the Commonwealth. The Commonwealth includes the United Kingdom, Australia, Canada and all countries that are or were controlled by Britain.

The Australian netball team celebrate winning Commonwealth Games gold.

Netball has been part of the Commonwealth Games since 1998, and is one of the only team sports to be included in the competition. In the Commonwealth Games competition, the netball teams are divided into groups of four. Each team plays the other three teams in their group and the winner of each group then progresses to the finals. The winners of the semifinals play each other in the gold medal match, while the losers compete for the bronze medal. Commonwealth Games athletes compete for their country, not just for individual glory or money.

Did you know?

Australian netballers Liz Ellis and Vicki Wilson have played more than 100 games each for their country. They have been part of a number of Commonwealth-Games-winning teams.

Glossary

arc   a curved path

attacking   trying to pass the ball down the court towards the goal or trying to shoot for goal

attacking positions   the positions of the players in charge of trying to get the ball into the goal circle to score goals, including the goal shooter, goal attack and wing attack

Commonwealth   a group of countries that are or were controlled by Britain

defensive   trying to stop an opponent from passing or shooting for goal

defensive positions   the positions of the players in charge of stopping the opposition from scoring goals, including the goal defence, wing defence and goal keeper

elite   the most skilful players who play in the highest levels of competition

goal   when the ball passes through the goal ring to score one point; also, the structure which includes the goalpost and goal ring

goal circle   the circular area around the goals at either end of the court

intercepting   catching a pass thrown to an opponent

lycra   an elastic, skin-tight fabric used in netball uniforms

obstruction   to stand closer than 90 centimetres to an opponent who has the ball

pivot   to swivel on the ball of one foot by stepping around in a circle with the other foot

shooters   the goal attack and goal shooter, who are the two players in a team allowed to shoot for goal

toss-up   when the umpire stops play and tosses the ball up between two players who have grabbed the ball or broken the rules at the same time; both players try to take possession of the ball